20 LIFE LESSONS FROM A
SOUTHERN BLACK MOTHER

Food
for
Thought:

COLLECTED AND SHARED BY
Nick Foulks

First Paperback edition September, 2024

Manufactured in the United States of America

ISBN: 979-8-9914720-0-5 (Paperback)
ISBN: 979-8-9914720-1-2 (eBook)
ISBN: 979-8-9914720-2-9 (Audiobook)

Contents

Introduction

Growing up as a black kid in a primarily white area I felt a lot like a zebra sometimes. I was black but painted with white mannerisms and characteristics. Even though I was surrounded by white culture I was not fully accepted. As I got older and ventured into the inner city to play high level basketball and found myself yet again on the outside looking in at a culture that said I didn't quite fit. It seemed even harder there, in the black culture, where I desired to be accepted. That desire for acceptance was strong but what was even stronger were the words and teachings of my family. Teachings that I learned crossed racial and cultural barriers because they were simply the realities of life. And these realities came into play whether you are dealing with white people, black people, brown people, or purple people eaters. It speaks to us all in some fashion.

We call it *Food for Thought*. The full expression would go something like this: "Baby, this is food for thought, take out of it what you need. Eat the meat and spit out the bones." Meaning, you may not agree with everything I'm about to say, but if there is something in it that can help you, then grab hold of it.

Over the years my mom gave me a lot of meat to chew on, if you will. She was from the south and you may not know this, but people from the south have a lot of sayings. Nuggets of truth that sometimes punch you in the gut and others that simply soothe the soul.

Many of these life lessons honestly have saved my life. They have given me peace, strength, hope, and courage. I hope they do the same for you. But again—take out of this what you need. It's just *Food for Thought.*

LESSON 1

Smelling like yesterday...

At first glance this may simply sound like a parent telling their child to take a shower before heading to school. But the meaning stretches much farther.

When I was young, I dealt with racial discrimination that hurt more than I liked to let on at times. But occasionally the frustration or anger would come through at home. My parents would try to strike a balance between talking to me about it and giving space to learn to deal with my emotions. However, when the frustrations or pain of a previous day would still be heavy come morning my mother would say,

"Don't start off today smelling like yesterday."

Meaning, what we may be carrying on us from previous days has the ability to funk up our current day. Learning to wash off what has happened, the past, prepares the soul for the goodness available on that day. However, if we want to wallow in the stench of our issues people will encounter the dysfunctional way we are seeing things. When we do this, we are engaging our future through the lens of our past. Similar to trying to drive a car forward while looking in the rearview mirror. Actions like that have a high likelihood of something bad happening.

> *Engaging new situations through the pain of a previous day sours the uniqueness of that moment.*

So how do we rinse off the funk of the previous day? The first step is acceptance of our frustration or pain. I remember when I was young coming through the doors of my home hurting but not willing to share or talk about anything because it felt like doing so gave power to the people who hurt me. But burying the raw emotions didn't help. Stopping to journal, writing a poem, or talking to the family forced me to articulate what I felt and why. After that I could make a conscious decision about how I wanted to move forward. I can keep swimming in the funk or shower off. The same is true for all of us. We can keep rinsing off the old and let people engage with the fresh us. Acknowledge the hurt, understand what and why, shower off.

REFLECTION

How many days have you gone forth smelling like the drama of a past day?

What did it cost you?

What is it costing you?

What if you have the power to change? To wash yourself in thoughts of love and thankfulness—to smell like hope rather than hate?

A steel tongue . . .

Have you ever said something you regretted? Of course you have! We all have! The question is what drove you to say it? When I was young, I had a combination of things that could get my butt into trouble real quick. Here was my winning recipe: good with words, witty (also known as a "smart ass"), and a short fuse. This combo more than once landed me in a place of regret. You would think that having two strong black parents with little tolerance for foolish behavior I would learn quickly. Well, you're wrong. It took me time to understand the power of this phrase.

"A steel tongue carries a level head."

What does that mean? Imagine trying to move your tongue if it was made of steel. Each word would literally carry weight! The amount of effort necessary to speak would give you pause to think about whether what you are about to say is worth saying.

Words have weight—think before you speak and you'll avoid regrets.

However, often we can get caught in our emotions and let our tongues run wild—to the point where others will say, and even we might say, *we lost our mind*, rattling off painful things or trying to prove a point at the cost of incalculable consequences.

My mother taught me over time that slowing down before you speak can keep you level-headed and in control of your emotions. While others are waiting for your comments or even hoping for you to lash out, you can weigh your words, keeping you level-headed and aware of the consequences of the next thoughts that leave your mouth.

REFLECTION

Where do you let your emotions run the conversation?

What would change in your world if you put this into practice? How would you speak to others if you truly understood the weight of your words?

What have you paid the price for because you let your tongue run wild?

Cinderella shoe . . .

It's amazing to see how many people live their lives in response to the issues of others. What do I mean? People have the ability to change your day, your week, your year, and even your life for good or bad.

Unfortunately, there are people out there who love to make their issues, mistakes, or drama somehow your issue. This is where my mom's wisdom kicks in.

"Put down that Cinderella shoe."

Cinderella was given a glass slipper by her fairy godmother that was custom designed for her to wear. When the prince goes looking for the owner of the glass slipper it becomes evident that it fits only one person. That's the same for issues of others that they are trying to make your burden. The shoe don't fit!

Those issues, mistakes, or whatever, belong to that person. So we have to stop trying to walk in their shoes. I don't know if you have ever put on someone else's shoes, but it just feels odd. And yet, we slide right into other folks' problems like they were custom made for us.

Others' problems aren't for you to take on.

We take on the emotions, complexities, and even repercussions that were not meant to be ours. This can happen for us in the work and home environment. Maybe it is a deep sense of empathy or a savior complex, but many people fall into this trap. The cost? Peace and perspective. We sacrifice our peace and lose perspective on a situation because we insert ourselves into it.

REFLECTION

Whose "shoes" are you wearing in life?

What causes you to do that?

What would change for you if you put that Cinderella shoe down?

LESSON 4

Lips weren't meant . . .

It doesn't matter who you are, at some point in your life you've found yourself trying to please other people at the cost of your own sanity. I get it! We all do it! Why? We want to be liked by other people, we want to fit in, we want to avoid conflict.

When I was growing up, and even as an adult, I found myself wavering back-and-forth between trying to be authentic regarding how I think and how I feel, but also toe the line. I think this is a reality for all of us. However, over time, if we fail to truly stand for what we believe in and what we hold as our own values, we lose something. We lose ourselves.

As a black female growing up in the time period that she did, and working in the geographical area that she did, my mother knew about toeing the line.

But she also knew that if you don't let people know where "your line" is, they will walk all over you.

I told you early on that I was the type of person who could cause trouble because of my short fuse. But over time I saw how the world worked. I became more and more aware of how I was viewed and what was necessary to blend. But when my frustrations would start to bubble to the surface, I could always count on Mama Foulks to hand me a plate with thoughts to chew on.

"Lips weren't meant to go that far down."

She helped me understand that no matter what you may fear the outcome to be, there comes a point where you need to make sure that you stand your ground and that your personal positions regarding significant issues are known. While kissing ass in life may get you to climb some type of ladder, at the end of the day, do you feel that you can respect the person you are, standing at the top?

Now I know this sounds like a big tough guy statement. Don't kiss ass for anybody! Make sure you give them a piece of your mind! But that's why it's important to go back to an earlier lesson: *A steel tongue carries a level head.*

It's not about giving everybody a piece of your mind or constantly drawing lines in the sand.

Rather it's about when you reach your threshold, you don't fold into a weaker version of yourself. Instead, with respect, you create a healthy boundary.

> *Hold to boundaries of your values and self-respect by speaking up for yourself when it counts.*

The big question is, how do you establish the boundary in a healthy way before losing your shit?

I think that's part of what isn't taught. It's easy to stay silent, it's easy to freak out. But being able to say, "Hey, I don't appreciate that." Or, "I can see why you would think that, but I don't agree with you."

It's like we operate either in compliance or conflict.

Here's the key: to operate with candidness. Candidness is being open, honest, and straightforward, but doing so with respect. In order for us to be candid, we also have to be confident about where we stand, and who we are. It's also about recognizing when we are no longer going to be a part of the herd culture but instead be true to our internal compass.

REFLECTION

Where in life might you fear creating healthy boundaries?

What is that lack of boundaries costing you?

Whose ass do you need to stop kissing?

Open hand . . .

Have you ever seen one of those movies where one person is hanging off the edge of the building or cliff and someone else is holding onto them? As you watch the scene it seems as though every time one person tries to hold on tighter, the other individual slips further and further away. This dramatic scene carries on until one character uses another hand to pull them forward. But other times, you watch as exactly what was most important to them slips through their fingers.

It's in our nature to dream for the first ending where we can rescue the things in our life by simply doubling down on our efforts. However, perhaps, if we're more realistic, we've seen the latter. Maybe it was a relationship where the more and more you tried to hang on, the further and further the other individual slipped away.

Or maybe it was the life that you wanted, and the more you tried to cling to it the further away it seemed. Perhaps it's the level of wealth that you desire—an ever-changing goal.

I know that I personally can relate to that. More than once I have found myself closing my hands around the things that I desire, unwilling to recognize the futility of my efforts. But freedom for me came when I took to heart this lesson. You have to:

"Learn to live life with an open hand."

We've all heard the saying that we came into this world with nothing, and we will leave it with nothing. That, my friends, is about as true as it gets! There is no U-Haul behind a hearse. When you come to the place of realization that everything is simply passing through your hands, that none of it is yours to keep, it changes things. Acknowledging the reality that every area of your life is actually not yours to control —whether it be finances, relationships, an occupation, or you name it—can be a hard pill to swallow.

Growing up, we didn't have a lot of money, but somehow my family always welcomed others into our home. Friends would come and eat up the pantry and drink up the fridge. I remember thinking to myself, how come my parents are okay with this? My mom was working four jobs at the time and my dad was working seventy-plus hours per week to make enough for us to just maintain.

When I asked my mom about it, she explained the principle to me. In her mind, God, the universe, or whatever you want to call it, was not in the business of blessing selfish people. It is important to see that nothing is yours. That meant things, money, and even people. A selfish or emotionally stingy heart in relationships was no different than a selfish and stingy heart about money.

> *Be generous with the time, money, and relationship you have now, knowing you really don't own them but just get to steward them.*

Your children are yours, but truly, you're simply stewarding their lives for a season. The money that you have, you are stewarding. The things you have, you are stewarding. If we become obsessed with clinging to it, we miss the gift of being generous, whether that be with physical things or our heart.

When we think about it, in all honesty everything we have in life is given to us for a season. The people we encounter, the money we have, the things we own, the dreams we aspire to. We are simply stewards of these blessings. It's important to recognize when that season has changed, when it's time to let whatever and whoever flow through our hands.

Who knows what financial breakthrough could flow into your hand when you stop clinging to your fear of not having enough? Who knows what relationship is out there waiting to come into your life if you can let go of the person who needs to flow out of your hand? Who knows what your kids can become when you trust that even when you release your grip, God will never release his?

REFLECTION

In what area of life might your hands be closed?

How would you feel if you were to release your grip?

What emotions come up when you think about it?

What needs to happen for you to release those areas?

What do you hope to happen if you do?

LESSON 6

When the heat wears off . . .

I don't know about you, but I'm gonna tell the truth and say I'm a sucker for romcoms. The combination of laughs and love story is something I find myself addicted to. The thing that always gets me about the storyline, however, is how quickly the relationships develop. I'll give you a quick breakdown of how it goes:

1. Random meeting with someone or long-term crush.

2. Physical attraction begins followed by passionate encounters.

3. Something happens to reveal a secret or issue that puts the relationship in jeopardy.

4. Cue the tear-filled keynote one-liner of the movie. Something like, "You complete me."

5. Big kiss, happy ending roll credits with scenes of a fun future together.

Got to love those films! Here's the thing: if you've ever been in a real relationship, you know that that sequence of events is full of crap. While numbers 1, 2, and 3 could possibly take place for you, there's no smooth one-liners to patch up the everyday struggles of real relationships.

Early on, because of the endorphin rush associated with this new relationship, we feel like our partners can do no wrong whatsoever. We are so attracted to them. We're so passionately in love with them. We're so excited to see them all the time. My mom calls this the season of the *heat*. It's the time in the relationship where you believe you're thinking with your heart, but the truth is you're thinking with your hormones. But just like a new-car smell wears off, so does the glitz and glamor of a new relationship.

It's crazy to think, but my mom was sixteen years old when she got married to my dad! He himself was only nineteen years old! She talks about how they were so in love, and she was willing to do anything for him. But guess what? They've been married for over forty-five years now. The new-car smell is long gone. I remember her telling me how important it is to be realistic in your relationships, because as you grow old with another person, "the heat" (*that hormonal endorphin rush that you feel, your sexual attraction towards another person*) ain't always going to be there. *HEAT is not what makes a relationship work; love does.*

> *"When the heat wears off that's when the love has to kick in."*

Too often today our world gets fixated on the romcom-like relationships we see in the movies. We're swiping to the left and to the right trying to find the person who sparks that flame in us all over again. We're staring at images of people on Facebook or Instagram showing their romantic moments and that makes us long for those "feels" all over again.

My mom taught me to look into the heart of a person and see what's in there. Because beauty will fade one way or another. It could be by age or by actions. Being vulnerable, authentic, and having open disagreements on the road to falling in love with who someone is will take us from heat to the heart. And once they have your heart and you have theirs, the love is what carries you through the different seasons.

> *Initial attraction needs to mature into loving the real person to sustain romantic relationships.*

When the body changes, when the circum-stances change, when the moments of pain hit, the love kicks in to see you through. But it's a choice we have to make. A pursuit. A mindset we choose—to move beyond the initial desire stage and press into the hard and real stuff. So that when the S H and all the I T hits the fan, love kicks in instead of anger.

REFLECTION

When in your life did you let the heat distract you from the heart of a person?

Have you ever felt like when the heat wore off in a relationship everything changed for you? What changed?

How are you moving from heat to heart in your cur-rent relationship?

Where do you need the love to kick in right now?

How can you invite your partner into that conversation?

Tongue and teeth . . .

If you've ever been in a serious relationship, then you probably had a serious fight with that same person. It doesn't matter whether we love somebody or not there comes a point where we're going to disagree. Sometimes those disagreements can be even stronger when we truly care about the person we're interacting with.

It's inevitable! And every time you meet a couple who seems like they've got everything together and they never fight, just remember they are lying. I'm not trying to judge; I'm just trying to keep it real. It's crazy how society will make you think that if you got the right person, you probably shouldn't argue with them. Everything should be hunky-dory, right? And as I talked about before, it might be that way for a season, but when lives come together, stuff gets complicated.

This perspective from my mom helped me put it in simple reality.

"It's tongue and teeth, baby, and it's all in there together."

Have you ever been eating something and you bite your tongue? I'm sure you have. And that jolt of pain is so horrendous. Because you weren't thinking about not biting your tongue at the time that you were eating, you were thinking about enjoying your meal. So when it happened, you were full-go on taking a big old bite. You weren't holding back.

Ever stop and think about how in the world that even happens? My mom would say it's because *it's tongue and teeth, baby, and it's all in there together.* And relationships are very much the same fashion. Here's what she means. In a relationship, all of who you are, and all of who another person is comes into play. It's not just the delicious savory parts of another person, it's the sharp edges, the grinding moments, and the sting of hurting the person you love.

You don't intentionally bite down on your own tongue when eating and oftentimes in relationships you are not intentionally trying to hurt the person that you hold close to you. But we have to realize when you're in close interaction with the whole person it's all in there together. All the emotions, all the insecurities, all the joy, all the past, and all their hopes for the future. So while you're enjoying the sweet taste of intimacy between the two of you, be aware that at some point in time you will unknowingly send a sharp pain through each other's hearts.

> *When we're in intimate relationships, we will unintentionally but inevitably hurt each other because we are a mix of both helpful and harmful habits.*

When you do bite your tongue, you don't just stop eating from that point on. Instead, you become aware of it, and if you recently suffered through that pain, you become more conscientious of how you're chewing. In the same way, when we hurt our partner, we have to be more conscientious of how we choose to interact with the person we love. Not because they are being too sensitive, but because we are being intentional.

REFLECTION

What tongue-and-teeth moments are showing up in your relationship?

How might things change if you stepped back and assumed the painful interaction was not on purpose?

How can you be more conscientious with your partner?

LESSON 8

Self shine…

In a world full of "likes" it's amazing how many people don't actually like themselves. Time and time again I meet people who, no matter how much they have accomplished, find themselves dissatisfied with where they are at. Well, there can be multiple reasons for this. One of the main sources I have found is our growing need for us as a society to receive external affirmation. Our social network-focused world has created a sense that if we don't post it and the world doesn't know about it, then it doesn't really matter.

Now I'm not saying we're creating a world full of narcissists, but I am saying we're not helping people move in the opposite direction. I'd be lying if I said that I am completely immune to the desire for others to appreciate, approve, or affirm the actions in my own life. For a long time I never felt like I was good enough—no matter how much I made in income, how many awards I won, or how much I achieved. Why? Because I needed to understand the power of personal reflection on my life.

Or as my mom would say it,

"Baby, you need to learn how to give your own self a shine."

Meaning, that you have to learn how to be proud of yourself. Why is this important? It's because no one but you knows the amount of time and effort, energy or sacrifice it took to accomplish whatever it is you accomplish in life. Nobody knows what it is you have gone through in the quiet times, in the times where you felt alone, and the times you didn't feel like you were enough, or the times when you really wanted to quit, but you didn't. Nobody can account for those moments behind the scenes except for you! And that's why when people want to affirm their accomplishments, it doesn't mean that much to us when they don't understand the action steps necessary to get to the goal.

Don't rely on external affirmation and approval without giving it to yourself.

If we're honest, sometimes the affirmations feel empty, hollow, or just not quite what it is we are looking for. It's because only your soul knows what you had to push through. So stop looking outside of yourself for others to give you confidence or approval.

You put the stamp of approval on you! You remember what you've done and gone through and give yourself a shine!

REFLECTION

What are a few things you have accomplished that YOU are proud of?

What would it mean to you to celebrate your journey?

How do you feel when you reflect on where you've been and what you've achieved?

Learn to follow . . .

Sometimes I feel like I'm the king of indecision. The fear of making the wrong decision can have a crippling effect for anyone. And that fear is often times of greater impact than the joy we might sense for making the right decisions in life.

But there comes different times in life when what we call a sixth sense, an inkling, or a gut feeling kicks in and we know the route we're supposed to take. But if you're like most humans, you don't always listen to that feeling. Instead, we seek the advice of other people, or we allow our doubts and fear to creep in. Suddenly, we're paralyzed, and we look for the route of least resistance. And while we feel safe for just a moment in the end, we suffer a sense of regret. Not because we made the wrong decision, per se, but because we in fact knew what the right one was and failed to pursue it.

When those moments happened to me in life, I would reach out to my mother and she would continuously reiterate to me,

> *"Baby, you have to learn to follow your first mind because your first mind is often your right mind."*

So what is the first mind? It's that voice inside of us that ushers us towards the decision, the change, the action we need to take that we know is in alignment with who we are. Why is this voice so powerful? It's because it's a voice of our true self. And that true self knows us better than anyone else. It knows our journey from start to present day and it knows what is in line with our values, our character, and our calling.

> *Trust your inner voice to give you the right answer.*

So why do we ignore it? I have found personally that in our humanity, it's natural for us to turn up the volume on the voices surrounding us, and turn down the volume on that internal voice. With so many surrounding inputs, how can we avoid the noise? The answer—stillness.

In no way am I saying ignore the wise counsel of others. Instead, I'm saying don't ignore the wise counsel within you. Finding time and space for stillness or practicing meditation allows us to empty out all the imposing thoughts of others, and align ourselves with the greater wisdom available to us.

REFLECTION

What are some times in your life where you have failed to follow your first mind?

What decisions are in front of you now that require you to turn down the volume of imposing thoughts?

What do you feel the greater wisdom inside of you leading you to do in those areas?

How can you make space for stillness and meditation in your own life?

Love is . . .

Three little words that have a huge impact, or at least they *used* to:

I . . . Love . . . You.

We hear it from our parents, our friends, in movies—and the list goes on. Heck, we have reality TV showing us love can be discovered in a week. But do we understand the weight those words should carry?

For a long time I thought that I did. I thought that the feeling deep in my soul, the desire that I felt, and the fact that the words continued to flow from my mouth were enough. I also was foolish enough to believe that the words coming from the mouth of someone else carried weight. But in love, like everything else in life, actions speak louder than words.

My mother told me when I was young,

"Love is what it does, not what it says."

People can say they love us all day long; but it's the actions they take that reveal the heart. How many stories do we hear of abuse laced with the words, "I love you?" Or a cheating partner who swears they love the person they have just wronged?

Our hearts can sometimes make us ignore what the eyes clearly see. We see a lack of care, kindness, or intimacy, but our hearts tell us love is there.

How can we be so confused? Often I think there are two drivers: fear and hope.

We hope that the way things used to be can be resurrected. We hope the person will come to their senses. We hope they will see our actions and reciprocate. So there we sit—on Hope Island.

Or maybe we fear. We fear that the lack of loving action is our fault. We fear starting over and finding a new relationship. We fear no one will ever love us. So we settle for less than real love.

Loving actions are evidence of the love between people, regardless of using the words.

On the other hand, what if we are failing to see the loving actions of someone because we are not receiving it in the form of words? There are times where you and I may miss the unconditional love of someone that flows through what they do consistently rather than what they say consistently. It's as though we can be blinded by the steadiness of their nature. The little things can be overlooked. We can become numb to the faithfulness of a partner.

We look for "tingles" and words when we should be looking for loving actions. So what do we do? First step: *slow down*. Take a moment to observe with honest eyes the relationships in our lives.

REFLECTION

What relationships in our lives currently exchange the words, "I love you?"

How are we showing up for others we say we love? How are they showing up for us?

What actions do we observe that illustrate the love someone has for us?

What actions can we take to show them love?

> "Dear children, let's not merely say that we love each other; let us show the truth by our actions."
>
> (1 John 3:18, NLT)

LESSON 11

Call a spade ♠ . . .

When I was a kid growing up, I loved to sit at the kitchen table late into the night watching my dad play dominoes with his friend Big Kenny. They would sit and trash talk each other because they knew how to play the game so well. Oftentimes, they knew exactly what was in the other person's hand.

The same thing would occur whenever my dad and I would be playing spades against anyone else. If you're not familiar with the game of Spades, it's a card game similar to hearts, but spades are the trump cards. The goal is to estimate correctly how many rounds your team can win versus the other team every time the cards are dealt.

The thing is, my dad taught me a lot about how to understand the game, count the cards in your head, and play the person across from you.

Sometimes you're setting people up by how you bid and looking to "set" them. Meaning you're able to take more rounds than they thought and causing them to go into a frenzy with each other. Now, it's fun sometimes to try to set people up but sometimes you have to call it like it is or you'll end up hurting your own team.

In the game, every time you underestimate how many rounds you can win, you're sacrificing points. That means the goal that you are trying to achieve (the win) continues to be out of reach because you're not being accurate about what is going on. Oftentimes the player is simply "playing it safe." But playing it safe by not correctly analyzing what's going on will cost you the game.

My mom referred to this when she said,

"Call a spade a spade."

I believe it's just in our nature to make things not seem as bad, or to make things even better than they may be—whether it be a relationship, our performance in our job, our bills, our finances, you name it—fill in your own blank.

What's the problem with that? The problem is we are distorting our reality. And that distortion may inhibit us from being grateful for what we have, from leaving a relationship or job that is unhealthy, or from change that needs to take place in our lives but can only happen when we see things as they truly are. Otherwise, you can end up messing up the whole game of life.

You have to learn to tell things like they are.

The reason people "play it safe" in Spades is about not being wrong. They fear the feelings that come with failing or loss. The same is true in life. We may not want to call out an unhealthy friendship, work situation, bad financial choice, or whatever, because we don't want to feel the impact of acknowledging reality. But what is on the other side of that? My mom would say that until you acknowledge *what it is, baby,* you can't make it into what it needs to be. Call it like it is and move on.

REFLECTION

Where in your life do you need to acknowledge reality?

Where have you played it safe or avoided the potential pain that comes from calling it like it is?

What would change if you started calling a spade a spade in your life?

Loaf of bread under their arms . . .

I'm always amazed how quickly we can become frustrated when listening to other people complain. But so often, many of us, including myself, are professionals at the art of complaining.

No sooner than we experience success in our lives, we can quickly find something else that is frustrating, irritating, or reducing the amount of joy we have.

"I'm glad that we got the house but I was so frustrated to find out that we needed a new furnace six months later."

"It's great that we have the ability to remain debt-free but I'm just frustrated with how much I have to work."

"I'm incredibly grateful for the bonus that I received, but I am so irritated by how much in taxes I had to pay."

Trust me, I am not pointing fingers whatsoever in this situation! I believe that I might have a master's, if not a PhD, in my ability to complain.

However, growing up, my mother was very quickly able to give me perspective on the frustrations I was enduring in my own life. She grew up in the projects of the inner city of Atlanta. Throughout her childhood, they experienced using candles because the electricity was turned off or having water with their cereal because they couldn't afford milk. So my frustration growing up on two and a half acres and never missing a meal didn't provide a lot of clout with her in regard to any complaints that I had. It's not that she was harsh about it, but she wanted to make sure that I understood the blessings that encapsulated the life I was living. Even today she continues to remind me that although I am experiencing difficulty, I need to recognize how blessed my life truly is. And when that time would arrive, she would remind me,

> "Baby, sometimes people can be crying with a loaf of bread under their arms."

In the world that is still filled with so many people who don't know where their next meal will come from, who have been sold into some type of sexual trafficking, or have to do unspeakable acts to survive, we should count our blessings. Please don't misunderstand me to be saying that your frustrations, your irritations, or your hardships are lesser simply because I'm comparing them to an extreme—that is not the point of what I mean. What I mean is, how can people who have endured concentration camps still see beauty in it? How can individuals who lived during time periods of slavery sing songs of praise? How can those who suffered disabilities or traumatic injuries smile and rejoice consistently? Perhaps, it's because they are recognizing the goodness that they are still holding onto.

Slow down and recognize the blessings that you're holding onto in light of the frustrations you may be experiencing.

If you were to stop and think about some of the areas where you find yourself complaining, what would those areas be? Now for just a moment, pause, and begin to name all the beauty that remains in your life. Think about the friendships you have, the meals you can eat, the fact that you are alive!

Our ability to stop and show gratitude can be the transforming mechanism that paints a new reality right before our eyes.

REFLECTION

What is a loaf of bread you are carrying underneath your arms that should allow you to rejoice in this moment, regardless of your circumstances?

Where can you stop allowing complaining to influence your perception?

How might life shift if you take a moment before complaining and recognize the beauty (loaf of bread) in your life?

Long handle spoon . . .

What do you do when people hurt you? How do you respond when someone continuously takes advantage of you?

Almost a decade, I worked in a full-time ministry role. During that period, I spent a lot of time teaching about the importance of forgiveness. Reality is based on the premise that each and every believer has been forgiven by God through the sacrifice of his son. So, operating from a place of unforgiveness seems to go directly against what Christian scripture teaches.

But before I was a pastor, I was the son of an old, southern black woman who taught me about letting go of my anger, but not being foolish in my relationships. It seems as though it can be very natural for us in society to operate from different extremes. One of the extremes would have us forgive and continuously trust that those around us have learned their lesson from the hurt they have caused us. So with that in mind, we can have an open conversation about what has happened and move forward in our relationship with them. Basically, we can give a mulligan for the relationship. The other side of the coin is pretty straightforward. You wronged me; you're dead to me. I'm sure a case can be made for both sides, and in fact, in a later life lesson, I will share about times to cut people off. But in this lesson, I learned about the importance of not creating unnecessary animosity between myself and someone else.

There are times in life where people are going to make choices that we don't agree with, they end up hurting us, or they show themselves to be someone we didn't realize was under the surface. When that happens, it doesn't mean we need to be immediately reactive, and cuss people out, but it also doesn't mean we need to simply overlook offenses and believe that a single conversation or two can reconcile what we have experienced.

I'll be honest, I am more along the lines of the "you wronged me; you're dead to me" mindset. I hate giving people energy from me who don't respect me or appreciate me or who've chosen to actively hurt me. It just seems easier to be done with any potential BS that could arise. But I think all of us know, we don't have that luxury in life to simply cut off anyone who hurts us. So what do we do?

> *"You have to learn to feed people with a long handle spoon."*

Have you ever been to the zoo or somewhere where they are feeding wild animals? Some of these massive beasts are incredibly dangerous. Now, while they are laying there watching you stare at them, they don't look like much, but when feeding time rolls around it's a whole new story. The trainers and zookeepers approach with caution and KEEP THEIR DISTANCE. They will still interact with the animal but they know how close they can get and remain safe.

That's the same way things roll out in life. There are people that you are going to need to interact with, and, while in certain situations they seem fine based on history, you are aware that they can wound you. Learning to remain calm but keeping the proper distance is key. What does this genuinely look like?

It's identifying the actions that are appropriate, but also protective when dealing with people who have hurt us in the past. For example, should you invite them into your circle with the hope that by being closer to you they won't hurt you again?

Nope. Should you be cordial when interacting while not sharing unnecessary additional information about your personal life? Yes.

Create the boundaries necessary to maintain your safe distance and self-respect.

Responding politely to a text or acknowledging them is not giving them power, it's actually maintaining your own. By simply keeping your distance, it shows that you are not going to give energy to this person beyond what is necessary. Going out of our way to let them know, "we are NOT good [on good terms]," shows that they impact you.

REFLECTION

Who in your life needs to be fed from a "long handle spoon?"

How have you currently been engaging with these individuals?

How have you felt using the method you are taking?

What would change if you created better boundaries?

What could those boundaries look like?

What emotions do you feel at the thought of implementing those boundaries?

LESSON 14

Snakes . . .

When I was young, my family would travel to Russellville, Kentucky, for our family reunion. It was always fun to meet my cousins from across the country and run around like crazy people as little kids. My parents would even let us drive their car through the open field. We played games, threw Frisbees, jumped rope, and did all the good stuff. One of the craziest parts about going to the family reunion was how they would clear space for the kids to play.

The home that we would go to was actually the original house for the Foulks family after slavery. This tiny home is nestled upon acres and acres of fields. But in order for the kids to go play the adults had to go clear the fields. What do I mean by "clear the fields," you might be asking? I mean, getting rid of the snakes hidden within the tall grass.

The older men of the family would walk the field, rustling up the grass, getting the snakes out, and shooting them if necessary. I know what you're thinking—*are you serious*? A hundred percent. As a kid playing in those fields, you had to be aware of your environment, making sure you watched your step and kept your ears attentive. It's not like the snakes were wearing signs that told us exactly where they were. Instead, they were nestled down, blending in with the surroundings, so making sure we were aware was critical.

I was fortunate enough to never encounter any snakes out in those fields, but I for sure have encountered snakes in life, as you no doubt have—whether it's in your work environment, your church—it can even be within your own family. There are times where you and I have to be watching our step and attentive to our surroundings because somewhere, blending into the crowd, are snakes, waiting to attack.

Okay, here's the thing: I'm not trying to be all doom and gloom about people. I'm just trying to keep it real based on what I've seen in my own life. Throughout my personal journey, there have been people who showed up one way for a season in my life, but given the right set of circumstances became a totally different version of themselves— a dangerous version—a version that's full of pain and venom. If I allowed it, they could bring resentment, anger, and pain. If you look back through your own life, I'm sure there are relationships that have turned from perfect to poisonous in a heartbeat.

Or maybe you encountered someone, and as you observed them you see tendencies that don't show the character you want impacting your world. Maybe it's a tendency to manipulate situations with gaslighting or telling half-truths to make themselves look better in given situations. Or perhaps it's how they treat others, their spouse, their coworkers, even their children. The issue for me is that people will continuously allow these types of relationships to remain in a place of influence within their world. But my mom always told me,

> *"If you find a snake in the grass you don't bring it in the house to bite you. Leave that shit where you found it."*

I remember reading a story about someone who owned a large boa constrictor and ended up being killed by the snake. I tried to understand how that happened. At what point did this individual stop acknowledging the danger associated with this snake? Think about it this way: if the same individual would've seen a boa constrictor that size in the wild, what might've been different about their mindset?

I assume they would've been more on guard and aware of the movements of the snake. And I doubt they would have taken that wild snake home. Because they had raised this snake from small to full adult they lost sight of the danger associated with the nature of that particular species.

The same thing happens to you and me when we bring snakes into our world. We consistently engage in relationships with people of low character and begin to grow numb to some of the dangers surrounding that.

> *You cannot bring or keep people close to you that show themselves to be untrustworthy or lacking character and expect not to get hurt.*

I've heard stories from people who are shocked that a "friend" had an affair with their spouse. But if they were watching closely, the promiscuous nature of that "friend" was constantly present. All it took was the right circumstances for that underlying nature to come forth. While it is important to be slow in judging other people, it's also important to look for the patterns. Very rarely do people truly change. More often it is the circumstances or situation that do not permit them to be who they truly are.

Once you begin to see how people act in varying circumstances or conditions, you can begin to come to conclusions rather than making judgments. However, when you come to the conclusion that an individual is of low character and dangerous, you now have a responsibility to leave that snake in the grass.

If you don't, then don't be surprised when they bite you.

REFLECTION

Who have you encountered in the past that turned out to be a "snake?"

What signs did you see in advance that could have prevented the pain you endured?

What, if any, relationships in your life have shown signs of potential snake-like behavior?

What behaviors have you identified in those individuals?

If their actions were to impact you in the way they have impacted others, how would you feel knowing you saw the tendency in advance?

What, if any, decisions should you make or precautions should you take?

Pride . . .

There are seasons in our lives where *the version of life we think we will have, the imaginary one* playing in our heads, is not unfolding the way we thought it would. My therapist taught me that this is called a *life script*. It's the version of life that we initially write and then we write it again and then we write it again. We don't end up in the ideal career right out of college that pays us a six-figure income. We don't end up with the white picket fence and perfect home. We don't end up with the 2.5 children and SUV (because minivans are not cool). Instead, we might find ourselves trying to figure out how we can manage our student debt and end up renting an apartment that our family barely fits in. We may have been unable to have children. Or we had more children than anticipated and have come to accept our minivan as a part of the family. The bills may be stacking up, the marriage may be falling apart, our teenage children may be acting in a way that doesn't seem to line up with who we know them to be. And we feel trapped in it; alone in it. On the outside, the world sees a family smiling for the Facebook feed, but on the inside we don't know how to change the course we are on. We want to scream for help but our words are swallowed up by the pride of life.

During those seasons, it can be tough to step into a place of vulnerability with those closest to us. The reason behind that inability to be open can come from many places. We could be ashamed of where we are right now. We could feel guilty about the circumstances surrounding our situation. We could fear creating a burden on someone else when life is hard enough for everyone.

It could also be that we just have pride. We don't want handouts or sympathy. We know what we are capable of and the sacrifice necessary to get through whatever is going on. Sure, it's not going to be fun or pretty as we go forward, but it is what it is.

Sound familiar?

That mindset of grin-and-bear-it runs deep in my veins, like a lot of people. When I was about thirteen, my mother was working multiple jobs and my dad worked as much overtime as possible to support the family. That being said, I found myself very often making my own meals. I learned to light the charcoal grill, fry chicken, work the oven, etc. I knew that if my parents could, they would be happy to make me a meal, but I also knew that they were giving all they had to keep us afloat. So it never bothered me.

Fast forward to high school and I am working as a cashier at Target on weekends, a janitor at the rec center behind our school after school, and as a bank teller half the day during my senior year. Three jobs while going to high school; to me it all seems normal.

Why is this my reality? Our family had fallen on harder times and we all pulled together to do our part. On the outside looking in, we never looked any different. We didn't wear our issues on our sleeves or our struggles as a woe, as some badge of honor—not our style. For us, it came down to doing what was necessary without making a thing about it.

By the time I reached eighteen, I had a deep-rooted sense of independence and very rarely, if at all, did people know any struggle that may be going on in my world. I had been trained that way. Not that my parents told me to never share your issues; but rather, it had been reinforced through what I experienced. But how many of us know that at some point, life is going to knock you to the ground, and as much as you try to pick your-self up your legs may just be too weak?

When I went through my divorce, that's where I found myself. Knocked to the canvas and lying on my back. The world spinning as I tried to process the repercussions on my kids, the financial pres-sure mounting, and the lack of self-worth compil-ing. This time . . . this time I couldn't seem to get myself back up. All I could think of was, "how could I let myself get here?" I knew early on life with this person was not going to work. Why did I keep going? When did I lose my independence? Why did I give in so much and so often? How could I keep bringing more kids into a broken marriage? Why did I think making more money would solve things? Why did I ignore the signs I saw?

Now, with all that spinning in my head—all the shame for not standing up for myself, for not walking away earlier, for getting into debt trying to please another person, and the guilt I felt for bringing four innocent children into this mess—how could I ask anyone for help?

One day, as I sat in my car on a video call with my family trying to hold it all together (thoughts still swirling), my eyes began to fill with tears and my body began to shake. My mother took one look and she knew. She knew I was not as okay as I had been trying to show. That's when she said to me, "Baby you have to let people in. You have to let people help you. You can only be strong for so long. And I know you have pride. We all have pride.

"There is pride and then there is foolish pride."

Right there I broke. I realized what she meant. Pride is a funny thing. It can give us strength but it can also cripple us. It can hold us hostage from the solution or the next step. That is what makes it foolish pride. Only fools ignore what could help them when they are truly in need.

If you are wandering in the desert, dying of thirst, and I have water that can help you stay alive, wouldn't you take it? Or would you say, "I'm the type of person who finds my own water, but thanks?" You would be a fool not to take the support that can save your life.

> *Our fear of how others will perceive us can shut down the very support the universe is trying to send us.*

At some point we come to the end of our ability to handle something. Because of mental, emotional, physical, or other reasons, the well has gone dry and we have nothing left. It's important we recognize that is the point where the strongest thing we can do is ask for help.

I needed help from my family in that season in multiple ways, and I also recognized I needed professional support. I needed to speak to a therapist and process all the swirling thoughts in my head and anger in my heart. I needed to lay down my pride and pick up my new potential future. To carry on alone would have been foolish.

But day after day we see families losing people they love to the pressure life can create. We see people trapped in their own thoughts and unable to see a way out. Inside they have reached the end of themselves and they think no one can help. Perhaps, they don't want to be a burden to anyone else and they start to believe it will be better if they are just gone.

That lie has cost so many people their lives. We can't close ourselves off from those who love us. We can't just use grit and bear everything in life. The script is ever changing and the story may not be what you want. But the disappointment or the shame doesn't have to become a cage that keeps you from help, love, and support for authoring a new version of your life. The vulnerability we fear is the very key that unlocks the door to our self-made prisons.

REFLECTION

Where have you allowed pride to stop you from being vulnerable?

Who can you safely invite into what you are going through?

How would you feel if you knew others cared and wanted to come alongside you?

What, if anything, would stop you from inviting them in?

How could professional help provide additional support to you in this season?

Daily bread . . .

When I was growing up, my family and I were not the church-going type. We didn't get dressed up on Sunday mornings, putting on our Sunday best to go listen to a sermon. But even though we weren't church-going, my mother could often be found playing gospel music in our home. Most commonly you would hear it playing on a Saturday while she was cleaning away and my sister and I were tasked with cleaning our rooms and bathrooms. I would joke and ask her if she's playing slave hymns, as we would be busy scrubbing toilets. Are you trying to connect to our roots? I would jokingly ask. She would often pull in scripture when we would find ourselves in a disciplinary situation, or maybe in a time of needing to push through a series of events. To be honest, it would often be a combination of scripture and a southern interpretation about life commingled together.

Oddly enough, in my early twenties, I would transition to a role as a pastor. Suddenly I found myself in a position of leading others spiritually, while at the same time growing in my own trust and faith in God. I don't know if you are aware of this, but young pastors are just above the poverty line. I often was working multiple jobs while serving as a pastor to make ends meet. Throw a kid or two into the mix and things can get real tight in the budget real quick. The tension for me came from watching other people around me grow financially while I seemed to be trapped in survival mode.

So many people going on vacations, getting promotions, buying beautiful houses—and the list goes on. This was before social media became prevalent and a place where discontentment is served to so many. I can't imagine how many people must struggle with feeling like they are behind as they watch people posting about all they have and do. If you are anything like most people, then making it all work can be enough to make you feel like you are forever running on a treadmill—no forward motion, just keeping pace.

After a while that can wear anyone down. We all have a desire to do more than survive. We want to excel! We want to see financial growth! We want to be able to indulge and enjoy the fruits of our labor!

But what do we do when we look up and we feel as though we are in the same spot? Do we focus on the lack of "forward progress?" Mama Foulks would say to me at that moment,

>   *"Baby, God promises daily bread, not a freezer-full."*

She is referring to a sermon Jesus gave in the book of Matthew. In the Bible, when Jesus is teaching his disciples to pray, he says, "Give us today our daily bread" (Matt 6:11). Jesus doesn't say, "God, at this moment, give us all that we need forever and always so that we feel totally confident about our future going forward." Nope. He says give us our *daily* bread. This indicates provision that can sustain us today.

Now I don't think any of us want to live hand-to-mouth. In fact, it's understandable that everyone wants to have a bank account full of money to spare. And that's not necessarily a bad thing. Financial margin can create a peace of mind for many of us. And it is healthy to save for rainy days. The problem arises when that becomes our focus point—when it becomes a stressor or a hindrance to enjoying life.

>   *The trap of needing more and comparison with others can block the appreciation for having enough for today.*

I will never forget talking to another man my age who I thought had it all figured out. He had the nice car, the house, traveled with his family, and the list goes on. When we sat down, I realized how much smoke and mirrors were at play. He was stressed and in debt. He wanted to provide all that he could and had become caught up trying to impress everyone around him. At this point it was all catching up and the bills were stacking up. He was grateful to just be able to cover the mortgage each month and knew that bankruptcy was a real possibility. His focus shifted from all he wanted to have and experience to suddenly being grateful for being able to meet immediate family needs. *Daily bread* was enough for him.

When I left ministry to start working in finance, the people I was around shifted, along with the lifestyles I was exposed to. Suddenly I felt so far behind. I saw people with massive amounts of money that I didn't think was possible. So there I was, feeling like I had failed. What choice did I have but to work like a mad man? And that is exactly what I did.

I reached a point where I grew so weary I craved a simpler life. I craved a life that focused on the gratitude of daily bread rather than never ending standards of "more." Maybe you can relate. So what do we do? Perhaps we stop focusing on building an unspecified amount of abundance and start with gratitude for what covers our needs. In reality, the cost of life today is often overwhelming enough. Have you ever stopped to think about how much it takes to keep your world going around? Even if you have made questionable choices in your spending that have increased your monthly expenses, stop judging yourself for a moment and start giving thanks that you can pay those bills! Sure we can all do better. But what if . . . what if we started by doing better at being grateful for what we have?

REFLECTION

What would change if you took time to give thanks for the ongoing provision you have in your life?

What would change if your focus shifted from more to more grateful for where you are now?

How can you create a practice of gratitude for what you currently have?

If you keep sweeping . . .

Some people love conflict and some people don't. Some people want to tell you exactly how they feel and some people won't. However, that natural tendency can change based on who is involved. Some relationships cultivate a condition of quiet. Meaning, we don't feel like we can say how we really feel.

Why not? Many reasons could be involved. Perhaps it could cost us a relationship, a promotion, a way people view us. And the thought of that level of loss we simply can't bear. So what do we do? We sweep it. We sweep it under the rug. We let it slide. We let it go—time and time again. We just keep sweeping. Another argument, another decision, another comment . . . What's the issue? My mom would say,

"If you keep sweeping shit under the rug it's gonna come out the other side."

Maybe you were thinking, *that's fine; at least it'll be out in the open then.* But that's assuming that whatever is coming out from under the rug comes out in a healthy fashion. Have you ever picked up a rug to see all of the compounded dirt and grossness that gets caught underneath there? It's not a pretty picture. As a dad of four kids, I can tell you firsthand it is incredible what you find, and incredibly gross as well. So if you have years of frustration swept under your emotional rug, do you think it's gonna be pretty under there? Doubtful. There are likely expectations, experiences, arguments, unacknowledged feelings —and Lord knows what else—waiting. So as it starts to come out, what does it look like?

At some point our actions or words are going to reveal how we really feel.

Maybe it's an out of character response to a common situation that has been bothering you. Perhaps it's an emotional disconnect from the person you keep sweeping crap for. Maybe it's just a look— a look worth a thousand words. Whatever the response, if it's flowing from under the rug, chances are it's not a good one.

Okay, where do we go from here? Start with getting honest, not with other people, but rather with ourselves. With whom and in what settings are we failing to express ourselves in a respectful manner?

Once we identify the people, then it's time to start thinking about what the triggers are. Maybe there are certain topics and certain settings that surround the interactions that fuel your frustration.

As you begin to lift the rug, give yourself grace. We are human. We get offended, angry, even bitter, but we also have the chance to take responsibility ahead of the eventual outburst, in whatever form it takes. Finally, what if the way you think the other person will respond is not accurate? Perhaps they are unaware. Fear can keep you captive for a while, but failing to be authentic can lock you in a version of you for life.

REFLECTION

When you think about the relationships in your life, in what areas might you be sweeping things under the rug?

For what reason do you find yourself doing this?

How might it be coming out the other side?

What might be a healthy manner for sharing your thoughts, frustration, or opinions surrounding these areas?

LESSON 18

Cry . . .

Growing up in the '90s and the early 2000s, the cultural influences I experienced are quite different from those of today. Whether I was listening to music or watching a movie, there wasn't a lot of room for emotional expression outside of anger, if you were a male. And even if you were a woman, the movies began to tilt towards the narrative of toughening up and not showing what it is you may be thinking or feeling. "It is what it is . . . The world is a mean, cold place . . . Nobody cares . . . work harder." Do any of these phrases sound familiar to you? Maybe you've heard that your tears aren't gonna change your reality.

Mental health is a topic that continues to sky-rocket in our society today. More and more people are having issues regarding the ability to manage their emotions and their feelings. So many of us grew up in a time or in situations that didn't allow us to fully express what it is we were thinking, feeling, or physically experiencing in our world. Culturally, we may be taught to shove things down or not show emotion in order to not be seen as weak. I know for me I grew up with the "only the strong survive" mentality. As I've shared before, my journey of growing up in a world where I didn't fit in made me feel like showing emotion was the same as putting blood in the water with a pool of sharks. As crazy as this sounds, I actually prided myself for not crying from third grade until my junior year of high school. No situation, whether it was pain or whatever, was enough to bring tears to my eyes after the death of my grandfather. And it wasn't until I blew out my knee and lost all my opportunities to play college basketball that I finally had tears.

The issue is that, although I never shed tears, I was ridden with a multitude of emotions during that time. And even as I grew older, I struggled to allow myself to feel some of the things that I was going through. Instead, I would place myself in a mental position to manage the things that I was going through, to deal with the things that I was going through, or to use the emotional energy I felt to power through.

And in my journey, I have met a lot of people just like myself who have done the same to manage what life throws at us.

But think about it this way: have you ever seen rescue workers trying to stop a flood? They pack in sandbag after sandbag to keep back all of the water. But the rain keeps coming and the pressure keeps mounting. Eventually, the sandbags give-away and the flood rushes free, causing devastation. Honestly, I think this is what happens to a lot of people when they have mental and emotional breakdowns. We've been putting sandbag after sandbag in place to help suppress some of what we're going through, but eventually that flood of emotions has to make its way out in some way, shape, or form. I personally have had my floodgate moments where everything burst forth, and I feel like I am spinning out of control, being swept away in the rushing waters of all the emotions that I have suppressed. But over the years, I've been able to take to heart the saying and lesson that my mother taught me.

"Baby, sometimes you need to just have yourself a good ass cry."

Hearing my mother, who always seemed to be tough as nails, share with me the importance of the tears she cried alone and how it brought healing to her soul changed my life. I had always seen her as this rock-solid pillar of strength that never broke, which was true, but she explained to me that,

Finding that point where you are strong enough to actually let it all out will help you rebuild the strength necessary to keep moving forward.

Think about it: when you truly let yourself have a deep cry, one that shakes your soul and lets out all of the unspoken words that you have held within, how do you feel after that? Is there a sense of deep release? Maybe it's a sense of sudden peace? Maybe it's a sense of acknowledgement? And what I mean is, that you have personally stopped to acknowledge the fact that you were feeling hurt or overwhelmed. Releasing the association of weakness or shame with feeling emotionally overwhelmed was a breakthrough for me in moving forward into what life has for me.

REFLECTION

When can you remember allowing yourself to have a good ass cry?

What were the circumstances that brought you to that point?

What area of your life right now do you need to acknowledge the emotional exhaustion you may be feeling?

How can you make space to allow yourself the emotional release you deserve?

Right will follow . . .

There's a lot of focus in our world today about the idea of karma, the universe, or sowing and reaping.

The premise is that what we put out into the world is what flows back to us. This means if we choose to put negative energy into the world through our words or our actions, we can expect negative results to flow back into our life. On the flipside, we can also expect that a positive mindset, or speaking positively into the universe may produce our desired results. Or maybe you have heard that if you and I can just get our vibrations at the right level, then the universe will align with us and all things will start to move the way we want.

Could it really be just that simple? Could we truly just think positive thoughts and live with positive energy, resulting in an amazing life that others can only dream about? I don't think I have enough scientific background to qualify as an expert on this type of subject matter. I don't have a PhD in quantum physics that permits me to talk to you about how energy patterns shift the world around us. What I do have are the gentle and real words of Mama Foulks,

"Baby, if you do right, then right will follow you."

The heart behind the saying is simple. It's not the complexity of the saying but rather the implementation of it that yields great impact. Speaking straightforwardly, it's very easy to say we should just "do the right thing." But how do we determine what the "right thing" is? What do we utilize to qualify things as right or wrong? Okay, you may be thinking I'm heading in the moral compass direction or perhaps I'm trying to create a foundation for utilizing some type of religion to ground you for right and wrong; but that's not where we're headed.

When you and I choose to do the right thing on a consistent basis then good things will result.

While all those things may be important in their own way, personally this saying has often been applied when I find myself caught between personal desires and selfless action. See, it's easy to look at a situation and go, "The right thing here is to not murder this guy who just gave me the finger while driving past me." Pretty straightforward.

What about a decision that forces you to delay your dreams so that someone else can succeed? What about a decision that causes you to sacrifice in order for something beyond yourself to move forward? What about a decision that forces you to let go of something you love because it's truly what's best? Now the way I position those questions makes it pretty plain and simple what the right thing to do would be. But I think all of us know the internal conversations associated with decisions like the ones forementioned are not cut and dry. There are mental and emotional hills and valleys we must travel in order to come to a conclusion. And if we are authentic, there's a good chance we haven't always made the right choice. We've made the right choice for us.

Please believe me, I'm not sitting in a place of judgment. I'm sitting in the crowd of those who have done that. But I've also sat in a spot where my soul feels a level of freedom because I made a choice that I know is truly right—not for me, but in light of what's best for the situation. And when that happens, many times something bigger, better, and greater has flown into my life. As humans, we naturally have what we think is right in any given situation. Why can't things go our way? Why can't it be simpler? Why should I have to make this type of sacrifice? I get it. But the more mature we can become at a 360-degree view regarding a situation, the better and better we become at doing right and trusting that the right will follow us.

REFLECTION

What are times in your life where you choose the right thing in light of personal sacrifice?

What happened after you made those decisions?

When have you failed to choose the right thing, but instead chose what you wanted?

What was the result?

What was the difference between those two situations?

What could empower you to choose right each time?

The pen . . .

The chapter on pride (*Chapter 15*) touched on life shifting and changing as time goes on. That, many times, life may not turn out as we *"planned"* it to be. Perhaps you're in a different career, live in a different state, are in a second marriage, had more kids than you thought, didn't have kids at all . . . the list really goes on and on. For example, when I was a kid, I was pretty sure my destiny was the NBA. I remember looking at Mark Price, a player for the Cleveland Cavaliers, who was a short white guy balling out. Then I saw Muggsy Bogues, basically the smallest guy to ever play in the NBA. Looking at those two guys, I thought to myself, *if they can make it in the NBA, I am for sure going to make it*. I'm already taller than them in sixth grade. This, my friends, was my first life script—my first projected version of what my life would be like. Then I thought I would go to law school but I ended up becoming a pastor. Queue the life script changes again. After I became a pastor, I thought I'll probably end up planting my own church someday. Nope. *Well, maybe since I started doing music I'll become a performing artist.* Negative. These are just the life scripts for my career. I can tell you that the life script in my head for family life, along with many other things, did not play as planned. I can assure you that my original life script did not include a life-changing injury, betrayal, divorce, depression, and a host of other negative aspects. Those, my friends, were all edits made to my original script.

In movies, there are edits and scenes that are deleted to create the appropriate timelines or because the scene didn't fit like the writer or director intended. What you and I witness is the finished product—a smooth film that makes sense. Have you ever wondered how it felt for the writer to see different scenes eliminated? Or for the actors who put in so much energy on a scene only to see it removed? I can imagine that there may be some emotions tied to that. But at the end of the day, the purpose is clear on why the edits are made. Unfortunately, that's not how life plays out. Many times the edits to our life scripts don't come with a clear understanding of how this edit improves the final result. But here is what my mom taught me:

"You hold the power of the pen."

There are times in our lives when it feels like everything is just happening to us. We are simply reacting to the changing environment or circumstances. Rather than feeling like we are in charge of the story, instead it feels as though we are spectators watching this movie play out, in suspense of what comes next—we have that feeling, that sense that we have no control. My mother taught me to slow my mind down from all of the swirling thoughts and realize that I don't have to simply react. Instead, I hold the power of the pen.

> *I have the opportunity to continue creating the life I desire, even though there are complications.*

I get to choose how to react to this situation. I get to choose where I will go from here. I get to choose what I'm going to believe about myself in light of what I'm going through. I may have lost a job, but I can write a story about overcoming this moment in my life. My body may have suffered a physical setback, but the story of who I become in light of that is up to me. Moving away from that victim mindset and into being the author of my journey mentality creates a sense of hope. While you may not be able to erase the pains of the past or the mistakes that you've made you can choose to pen out a story of growth, gratitude, and hope.

REFLECTION

Where in your life have you seen a change in your life script?

How did you respond when that happened?

Looking back, how have you grown from that change?

Where are you currently seeing a change in your life script?

What would change in your mindset if you took on the power of the pen mentality?

Remember, that same opportunity to grab the pen and write a new chapter is before you today and every day.

Final Thoughts

There you have it! A full plate of food for thought. I hope you were able to eat the meat and spit out the bones. These are just a few of many more lessons that Mama Foulks has shared, but it's a good start. As the wise words of Mama Foulks now echo somewhere in your subconscious, I hope they give you comfort and courage. I wrote this book to honor her. The wealth that she has given me in life lessons far outweighs any other form of inheritance I could receive.

I'm sure that as you reflect on your own family, you too can hear the words of wisdom that have guided you through your own journey. Every family has *Food for Thought*. I want to encourage you to capture those phrases and lessons so that generations to come will know the hearts of those who may not be alive today. There is so much beauty in the words of those we love.

As an additional resource, I have created the *Food for Thought Journal* to help capture your own reflections and personal family's recipes for wisdom. You can find it at www.nickfoulks.com.

About the Author

 Nick Foulks is an author and Certified Professional Life Coach with 20 years of professional speaking experience. He has also created a successful career as a top sales performer. He is passionate about helping others unlock their full potential, whether they are aiming to elevate their career, boost their sales performance, or find renewed motivation. His life coaching skills, complemented by his deep experience in speaking and sales, allow him to offer practical, relatable guidance to help others succeed. He resides in Wisconsin with his four children.

www.ingramcontent.com/pod-product-compliance
Lightning Source LLC
Chambersburg PA
CBHW070438130626
46553CB00006B/2236